Religious Extremism

Otto James

Evans

TITLES IN THE VOICES SERIES:

DRUGS ON THE STREET • GANGS • RACE HATE

RELIGIOUS EXTREMISM • VIOLENCE ON THE SCREEN

Published by Evans Brothers Limited
2A Portman Mansions
Chiltern Street
London W1U 6NR

First published 2006
© copyright Evans Brothers 2006

VISIT OUR WEBSITE
Evans
www.evansbooks.co.uk

British Library Cataloguing in Publication Data
James, Otto
Religious extremism. – (Voices)
1. Religious fanaticism – Juvenile literature
I. Title
306.6

ISBN 0 237 52721 9
13-digit ISBN (from 1 January 2007)
978 0 237 52721 1

Editor: Susie Brooks
Designer: Mayer Media Ltd
Picture research: Sally Cole and Lynda Lines

Produced for Evans Brothers Limited by
Monkey Puzzle Media Limited
Gissing's Farm, Fressingfield
Suffolk IP21 5SH, UK

Picture acknowledgements
Photographs were kindly supplied by the following:
Alamy 8 (Paul M Thompson); Art Archive 10 (Museo
del Arte Antiga, Lisbon/Dagli Orti), 12 (University
Library, Geneva/Dagli Orti); Empics 6 (Rajesh Kumar
Singh/AP), 18 (AP), 26 (Carmen Taylor/AP), 28 (Mark
Humphrey/AP), 33 (PA), 34 (AP), 39 (CP Canadian
Press), 43 (Aman Sharma/AP); Getty Images front
cover, 9 (David Hume Kennerly), 14 (Anja
Niedringhaus/AFP), 16 (Pius Utomi Ekpei/AFP), 17
(AFP), 25 (Romeo Gacad/AFP), 27 (Spencer Platt), 30
(Joe Traver), 35 (Shelly Katz), 36 (Asahi Shimbun/AFP),
38 (Robert Nickelsberg), 42 (Oleg Nikishin);
Popperfoto.com 13; Reuters 1 (Abed Omar Qusini), 21
(Abed Omar Qusini), 24 (Jerry Lampen), 29 (Susana
Vera), 31 (Charles W Luzier), 37 (Toshiyuki Aizawa), 40
(Thaier Al-Sudani); Rex Features 5 (Israel Sun), 7, 15
(Action Press), 19 (SIPA), 23 (SIPA); Topfoto.co.uk 4,
11, 20, 22 (Ilyas Dean/Dean Pictures/The Image
Works), 32 (Fujiphotos/The Image Works), 41 (Peter
Hvizdak/The Image Works).

CONTENTS

WHAT IS RELIGIOUS EXTREMISM?

'Religious extremism' describes anti-social behaviour that is based on religious beliefs. Sometimes people's extreme religious views make them treat others as inferior or wrong. Extreme religious beliefs can lead to violence.

Strong views

People with strong religious beliefs often want to force their view of the world on others. They feel that only those who follow their 'true' religion should be able to make important decisions. For example, the US Christian leader, Reverend Pat Robertson, claimed in 1985:

❝ No one is fit to govern other people unless first of all something governs him. And there is only one governor I know of that is suitable to be judge of all the universe – that's God Almighty. ❞

Muslim women protest against a book called *The Satanic Verses*. They wanted the author, Salman Rushdie, killed because they believed his writing insulted the Islamic religion.

Suicide bombing – where someone blows him or herself up in a public place, deliberately harming others too – is used by extremists all over the world. This explosion on a bus took the lives of the bomber and many of the passengers.

Long-running conflicts

Sometimes extremists decide to use violence to enforce their view of the world. They attack those who think differently, especially if they voice opposing opinions. This intolerance of other people's views can lead to long-running conflicts. Dr Mahathir Mohamad, prime minister of Malaysia, said in May 2001:

❝ Intolerance breeds injustice [unfairness]. Injustice invariably leads to rebellion and retaliation [revenge attacks], and these will lead to [increased violence].... Once started, religious strife has a tendency to go on and on, to become permanent feuds.... Always the extremist elements invoking past injustices, imagined or real, will succeed in torpedoing the peace efforts. ❞

"The potential for violent conflict... exists when our beliefs command us to do something aggressive to another group... like take their land because we believe our deity [god] promised it to us."

Dan Smith in *The State of the World Atlas*, 2003 edition.

WHAT MARKS AN EXTREMIST?

Religious extremism and violence are part of many religions. But does that mean everyone whose religious behaviour seems extreme must be an 'extremist'?

Holy sacrifice

In India, holy men walk the roads, begging for food and other things they need, with few possessions of their own. They hope that living an extreme lifestyle will show their devotion to their religion. In his book *The Razor's Edge*, the writer Somerset Maugham describes such a holy man:

❝ I looked round and saw a bearded man with long black hair, dressed in nothing but a loincloth, with a staff and the begging-bowl of the holy man.... He said he was making a pilgrimage on foot to the holy places of India. ❞

To most people, living like this might seem extreme – but it does not necessarily make the holy man an extremist.

A Hindu holy man prays at one of India's many holy sites. The holy men live in extreme poverty, travelling from site to site, because of their devotion to religion.

"No religion is free from extremism."

Abdelfattah Amor, United Nations Special Reporter on Religious Intolerance.

This London bus was destroyed by Muslim bombers on 7 July 2005.

Extreme action

In contrast, the four Muslim extremist suicide bombers who killed themselves and 52 innocent people in an attack on London in July 2005 were said to have lived normal lives. A neighbour of one of the bombers, Mohammad Sidique Khan, said:

❝ He didn't seem to be an extremist. He was not one to talk about religion. He was generally a very nice bloke. ❞

Some commentators have asked whether religion was the real motivation for the attacks. They suggest that the bombings could, for example, have been a protest against British and US actions in Afghanistan and Iraq.

Whatever the truth of this, on 7 July Khan detonated a bomb on a London Underground train that killed seven people. This behaviour marked him and his fellow bombers out as extremists.

WHY DO PEOPLE BECOME EXTREMISTS?

Not everyone who follows a religion is an extremist – most are just ordinary people. So what is it that causes some people to take an extreme view of their faith?

Group support

Andrea, from the UK, joined a religious group because she felt welcomed and supported by its members:

❝ I grew up in a Christian environment but in my teens I found that if you were too happy it was labelled 'irreverent'.... When I first came here [to the church group] I felt accepted as I was for whoever I was or tried to be. I was amazed that in front of such a large group of people I was, and still am, free to be myself. ❞

Many religious groups promote themselves and recruit new members on the streets. This bus is owned by the Christian organisation the 'Jesus Army'.

Isolated ideas

However, some people who join religious movements end up isolated from their friends and family. One woman in the USA discovered this when her daughter and a friend went on a religious course:

❝ She came back criticising her parents because they had normal jobs instead of being missionaries. She married one of the guys from the course, and they went to be missionaries together. ❞

Once people are isolated, they become more likely to act in an extreme way. Kamal, who once belonged to a Muslim extremist group, remembers:

❝ You don't have your mum and dad or brothers or sisters there saying, 'No, Kamal, that's not a fair way to act'. So it's much easier for them to persuade you to do this or that because, they say, the Koran [Qur'an] says you should. ❞

More than 900 people died when their Christian cult leader persuaded them to commit suicide in the isolated community of Jonestown, Guyana, in 1978.

"There is no more powerful ally one can claim in a debate than Jesus Christ, or God, or Allah, or whatever one calls this supreme being. But like any powerful weapon, the use of God's name on one's behalf should be used sparingly."

US Senator Barry Goldwater.

IS EXTREMISM A NEW THING?

Religious extremism is often mentioned in today's news – but it is not just a modern problem. World history is studded with religious disputes that have cost millions of people their lives.

Ancient conflict

Muslim Arabs, or 'Moors', once controlled Spain. Between AD 727 and 1492, Christian forces battled to win control of Spain from its Muslim rulers. Thousands of people died in the fighting. The Christian leaders were quick to tell their troops that God was on their side. As Archbishop Diego Gelmírez of Spain said in 1125:

❝ Let us... become soldiers of Christ and [defeat] his enemies, the evil Moors. ❞

Later, in the fifteenth and sixteenth centuries, Christian Spanish soldiers – known as *conquistadors*, or 'conquerors' – fought battles in newly discovered countries in South America. They thought that St James (the patron saint of Spain) was on their side, fighting against the local people. Because the locals were not Christians, the *conquistadors* felt justified in killing them, and in taking their land and possessions.

Muslims ruled successfully in Spain from the early eighth century until the late fifteenth century, having been invited to enter the country by one of its Christian leaders. This painting shows a later battle between Christian and Muslim forces.

Country divide

Another example of religious conflict happened in 1947 when India and Pakistan, previously united under British rule, suddenly became independent countries. Pakistan was mainly Muslim, India mainly Hindu. Many people were caught on the 'wrong' side of the border between the two countries. Distrust and hatred between Hindus and Muslims erupted into violence:

❝ The... massacres left at least one million dead, with the brunt of the suffering borne by the Sikhs who had been caught in the middle. ❞

Train stations saw some of the worst scenes. One report described what British officials found as they arrived at Lahore station:

❝ On the platforms [they] found the railway staff grimly hosing down pools of blood and carrying away piles of corpses.... Minutes earlier a last group of desperate travellers had been massacred by a... mob as they sat waiting quietly for the Bombay Express. ❞

Crowded trains bring Hindus from Pakistan to India in 1947. At least 10 million Hindus, Muslims and Sikhs fled their homes, most of them travelling by rail.

"When I grew up I was shocked to learn that some of my neighbours were not the real owners of their houses. The real owners had been forced to leave.... The violent and fratricidal partition [of India] forced many Hindu families out of my country to seek refuge in India, on the other side of the border. At the same time, many Muslim families left India, and came over to my country. I heard that it was religion that led to all these disasters. When I was young I could not understand what type of religion that was."

Taslima Nasrin, Bangladeshi human rights campaigner.

CHRISTIAN EXTREMISM

A number of religions have followers whom other people call 'extremists'. Christianity, for example, has a long history of extremism, dating back hundreds of years.

'False believers'

The medieval Christian church wanted to make sure all Christians followed the same beliefs. Those who disagreed were called 'heretics' (people who preached a false religion). Some heretics were punished by being burned at the stake. One was John Hooper, Bishop of Gloucester, who died a horrible death in 1555 in front of 7,000 spectators. The writer Henry Moore reported:

❝ The command to light the pyre came... a fierce fire built [but] Hooper remained alive.... More tinder had to be brought as the fire died down.... Now the whole of the lower part of his body was burnt away, and then his guts burst... shortly after, he keeled over and fell into the embers.... It took almost an hour for the bishop to die on the pyre. ❞

"It is rating one's conjectures [theories] at a very high price to roast a man alive on the strength of them."
Michel de Montaigne (1533–92), French writer and philosopher.

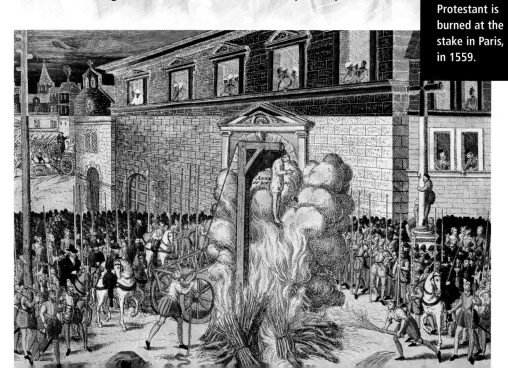

A French Protestant is burned at the stake in Paris, in 1559.

Members of the Ku Klux Klan attend a meeting. Despite their comical appearance, Christian Klansmen murdered many black Americans, especially in the USA's southern states.

'God's chosen race'

In the nineteenth and twentieth centuries, an extremist 'Christian Identity' movement began to blend Christianity with racism and anti-Semitism (hatred of Jews). Its philosophy centred around the belief that white people are God's chosen race. In southern US states, Christian Identity groups including the Ku Klux Klan carried out lynchings of their enemies. According to Dr Arthur Raper, writing in 1930:

> **3,724 people were lynched in the United States from 1889 through to 1930. Over four-fifths of these were [black]. Practically all of the lynchers were native whites.... A number of the victims were tortured, mutilated, dragged or burned.**

According to the FBI, today's Christian Identity followers believe they are:

> **...the last line of defence for the white race and Christian America.... They engage in survivalist and paramilitary training, storing foodstuffs and supplies, and [storing] weapons and ammunition.**

CAN POLITICIANS CAUSE EXTREMISM?

Some politicians have been accused of using religious feeling for their own advantage. There are examples of this in India, Pakistan, Central Europe, North Africa, Israel and many other places.

From harmony...

In Bosnia, Muslims and Christians once lived peacefully side by side, as Zahid Olorcic remembers:

❝ Funerals, weddings, birthdays, we never counted how many Muslims were there, how many Serbs, how many Croats. The only important thing was to be together, to have fun, to drink a little. It had been like that for so many years I never suspected it could change. ❞

Things *did* change, though, when Christian Serbian politicians began to whip up hatred for Muslims.

The Serbian politician Radovan Karadzic, using a map to explain to journalists how Bosnia is divided between different religions and cultures.

... to hatred

The Serbian politician Radovan Karadzic told a newspaper at the time:

❝ We know Muslims and Serbs do not want to be together. The international community and the Muslims must accept this country used to be totally Serbian. ❞

Soon after, Serbian forces began to expel Muslims from 'their' territory. A vicious war started and thousands of Muslims were killed. Karadzic's old neighbours, many of them Muslims, could hardly believe what was happening:

❝ It is a mystery.... Half of our neighbours are dead now [because of him], and most of them were Karadzic's first neighbours. He talks now about being unable to live with Muslims. [Back then] Muslims helped him the most! ❞

The United Nations decided that Radovan Karadzic was responsible for war crimes. In November 1995 he was charged with genocide. He was also charged with putting thousands more Muslims in concentration camps.

In Bosnia's capital, Sarajevo, the old Olympic Stadium had to be turned into a cemetery for victims of the war.

"I believe in an America that is officially neither Catholic, Protestant nor Jewish... where no religious body seeks to impose its will directly or indirectly upon the general populace or the public acts of its officials."

John F Kennedy, US president 1961–63, explaining that he did not think religion and politics mixed.

DOES POVERTY CAUSE EXTREMISM?

Religious extremism is sometimes linked with poverty. Poor areas – from the Middle East and Asia to the US, the UK, Spain or Germany – are all home to extremist groups.

Hope for the poor?

There are people all over the world who live in poverty. They have hardly any money, unhealthy living conditions and little food. It is hardly surprising that they are keen to hear about other ways of living. One writer notes:

" Stroll through Nairobi, Kenya's capital, during any lunch hour and you will see throngs of poor people listening to unkempt prophets stridently preaching hope. "

And as a Christian man in Kenya, Moses, says:

" When you cannot feed your children, when your pay is less than the money you must spend to live, it is hard to believe in the way the world is. I prefer to believe in another world, one made by [God], not men. Maybe that world only exists when we die, but it must surely be a better place than this. "

In 2004, Nigerian Christians launched attacks on local Muslims. After Muslim retaliations, some Christians had to take shelter in this church – which ironically bears a sign about a 'Love Crusade'.

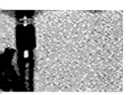

Dangerous wealth

On the other hand, some religious extremists are very wealthy. One example is Osama bin Laden, a Muslim extremist leader. Bin Laden is thought to be responsible for many terrorist attacks by Muslims:

❝ Officials in many countries including the United States say that bin Laden's money has paid for attacks in Europe, Africa and the Middle East. His personal wealth is estimated at US$ 250 million. ❞

Other religious extremists have also come from wealthy families. This suggests that even if poverty is partly responsible for extremism, it is not the only cause.

The millionaire Muslim extremist Osama bin Laden. Bin Laden comes from an extremely wealthy Saudi Arabian family.

WHO OWNS THE LAND?

Around the world, many religious conflicts are linked to a battle for land. Sometimes these battles have been raging for centuries, with two or more religions claiming the land is 'theirs'.

Tamil tensions

The population of Sri Lanka is roughly 70 per cent Buddhist. There is disagreement between the Buddhists and Tamil people, who are mostly Hindu. Hindu leader Kandiah Neelakandan says:

66 Even in Colombo [Sri Lanka's capital], Tamil children feel there is no hope for their lives. They all want to go abroad, because there is nothing for them here. 99

Many Tamils who want their own country support the Tamil Tigers, a terrorist group. Although the Tigers reject all religions, the conflict is rooted in differences between competing religions. One Tamil boy says:

66 The [Tigers] are... fighting to create an independent homeland, and we also want this, because it would mean freedom. 99

Young Tamil Tigers at a training camp in Sri Lanka. The Tigers were one of the first groups to use suicide bombing as a means of attack.

This Croatian woman stands outside her ruined home, destroyed by a huge bomb planted in a truck.

DYING OVER RELIGION

Violent deaths, until 1999, in areas where there are religious conflicts:

Chechnya	5,000
East Timor	200,000
India/Pakistan	30–70,000
Kosovo	18,000
Sri Lanka	60,000+

A.J. Jongman, 'Downward Trend in Armed Conflicts Reversed'

Continuing conflict

The conflict in Sri Lanka has cost many lives. It spills over from one generation to the next. One 12-year-old Hindu boy whose parents had been killed in the fighting said:

We would like to avenge the deaths of our parents by assaulting the soldiers who did it.

Does religious conflict always have to carry on through the generations? In Bosnia, tens of thousands of people died when Christian Serbs fought Bosnian Muslims and Christian Croats for the land. Lana Obradovic is a student from Bosnia. Her father, grandfather and cousins died during the religious conflict. She says:

The war changed everything in my life and I was one of thousands forced to leave during the ethnic cleansing in my city. But they did not manage to change me. I have NOT learned to hate my neighbours and I never will.

WHO OWNS ISRAEL?

One of the oldest religious conflicts about land continues today in Israel. Here, fighting between Jews and Muslims has been going on for a century. The modern version of this dispute began with the birth of Israel in 1948.

Driven out

In 1948, the land that is now Israel was to be divided between Jews and Arab, mainly Muslim, Palestinians. But the Palestinians refused to accept this, because most of the 'Jewish' land had been lived in by Palestinians for generations. In the war that followed, Israeli Jews took over much Palestinian territory. One report stated:

" 700,000 Palestinian refugees were forced to leave their homeland immediately before, during and after the war, the lucky moving to different Arabic countries, the rest interned in camps. This has only bred more conflict. "

Palestinian refugees arrive in Gaza in 1949, fleeing from the fighting. Many refugees are still living there, almost 60 years later.

"Victory in the War of Independence, glorious as it was, cost us 5,000 and more of our precious lives. But if ever Jewish lives were not lost in vain, it was then."

Israel, Years of Challenge by David Ben Gurion (Israel's first prime minister).

Violence on both sides

Since 1948, the Palestinians have been trying to regain their land. Violence on both sides is now common. Muslim groups, for example, use suicide bombers to attack Jewish targets. The father of one suicide bomber said:

" I am very happy and proud of what my son did.... [He was] very religious since he was young; he prayed and fasted. "

Many ordinary people on both sides are sick of the situation and wish the extremists would stop. One woman declares:

" No cause, however moral, can justify blowing up civilian people celebrating... in a hotel, or people sitting in a cafe... "

These Palestinians are trying to keep back an Israeli Army bulldozer that has come to destroy their homes.

BOMBER FACTS

Of the suicide bombers in Israel:

- 47% have an academic education and an additional 29% have at least a high school education
- 83% are single
- 64% are between the ages of 18 and 23; most of the rest are under 30
- 68% have come from the Gaza Strip.

In September 2005, Israel began to evacuate its people from former Palestinian territories in the Gaza Strip. Many hoped this would help to bring about more peaceful relations between the communities.

IS EXTREMISM FUELLED BY WORLD POLITICS?

Some people feel that religious extremism is caused or encouraged by the actions of the world's governments. Some even claim that the actions of a government in one country cause extremism to grow elsewhere.

Blaming America

In 1998, an Arabic newspaper stated in an editorial about Muslim attacks on non-Muslim targets:

❝ One should not be surprised by the attacks and the anti–American violence. The Americans are the ones who created this violence and utilised it for a long period of time. They have no one to blame but themselves. ❞

Many Muslims feel that the USA supports the Israeli government. The Israeli Jews use violent tactics to keep control of Muslim Palestinian areas. Why, Muslims argue, should it be a surprise when supporters of the Palestinians fight back against Israel and its ally, the USA?

Muslims burn an American flag at an anti-US/UK protest in Karachi, Pakistan.

"The US government has committed acts that are extremely unjust, hideous and criminal through its support of the Israeli occupation of Palestine."
Osama bin Laden, May 1997 interview with CNN.

"Some Muslims [see] their own governments... as corrupt, oppressing their own peoples, and selling out to false Western ideals. US support for these regimes is sometimes seen as a cynical exchange for access to energy resources and military basing rights."

Anti-American Violence: An Agenda for Honest Thinking by C Richard Neu of policy advice group RAND.

The aftermath of a Muslim bomb attack on the Hindu island of Bali, in which hundreds of people died. Bali was targeted because it was a popular holiday destination for Westerners.

Revenge attacks

One Muslim claimed that the USA's actions abroad:

❝ ...can only stir hatred for America and Americans, and this is what is happening from the far east to the far west. Every day we witness [violence] against US soldiers, civilians, companies, restaurants, military bases, and all the security measures cannot prevent this. ❞

When Muslim terrorists set off suicide bombs in London in 2005, British MP George Galloway was among those who felt that international relations were partly to blame:

❝ We argued, as did the security services in this country, that the attacks on Afghanistan and Iraq [where British forces supported US-led invasions of Muslim countries] would increase the threat of terrorist attack in Britain. Tragically Londoners have now paid the price of the government ignoring such warnings. ❞

ARE MUSLIMS TREATED UNFAIRLY?

Muslim extremists – from Afghanistan, Iraq, Iran, Indonesia and elsewhere – get lots of publicity. It can seem that all Muslims must be extremists because of their strong beliefs. Is this really the case?

Dutch people hold up images of Pim Fortuyn, the politician known for his strong views on immigration, who was murdered in 2002.

Strict Sharia

The Qur'an – the Islamic holy book – lays down strict laws called Sharia laws. These laws form an important basis for Muslim culture. One Dutch Muslim says:

❝ The Sharia does not have to adapt to the modern world because these are divine laws. People have to bend to the Sharia. ❞

Many Muslims feel that Sharia laws should be universal – obeyed by everyone. As a British source reported:

❝ In London, Sheikh Omar Bakri [a Muslim leader] openly declared his intention... to establish Sharia on British soil. 'I want to see the black flag of Islam flying over Downing Street', he said. ❞

But many non-Muslims say that the restrictions of Sharia laws cannot fit with the freedoms of the West.

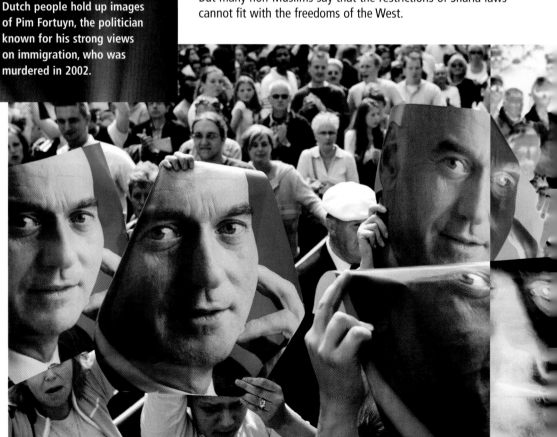

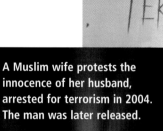

A Muslim wife protests the innocence of her husband, arrested for terrorism in 2004. The man was later released.

Misunderstood?

Some political leaders feel that Muslims and their values play an important part in society. According to US President George W Bush:

“ Muslims make an incredibly valuable contribution to our country. Muslims are doctors, lawyers, law professors, members of the military, entrepreneurs, shopkeepers, moms and dads... they need to be treated with respect. ”

Even so, many Muslims fear that they are tainted by the actions of a few extremists. After the suicide bomb attacks in London in 2005, one newspaper reported:

“ [There are] growing fears that British Muslims face violent reprisals for the bombings, which have killed more than 50 people and wounded another 700. ”

This was despite the words of the general secretary of the Muslim Council of Britain:

“ Those behind this atrocity aren't just the enemies of humanity but enemies of Islam and Muslims. The people on the receiving end of this, both as victims of the bombings and victims of the backlash, are Muslims. ”

DISCRIMINATION?

In 2003 the Council on American-Islamic Relations reported that anti-Muslim feeling was increasing steadily:

● In 2003 there had been 602 complaints of discrimination.

● This was a 15% increase on 2002, and a 64% increase on 2001.

WHAT DRIVES AL QAEDA?

Al Qaeda is the most famous Muslim terrorist alliance. Very few people would argue that it is not extremist in its attitudes and methods. But what are its motives?

Part of the Al Qaeda attack on the World Trade Center in 2001, after an aircraft had been flown into the skyscraper.

9/11 FATALITIES

Number of fatalities in the 11 September 2001 attacks on the USA

World Trade Center	2,595
Flight 11	92
Flight 175	65
Pentagon Building	125
Flight 77	64
Shanksville Flight 93	45
Total	2,986

'Protecting Arabia'

Al Qaeda is led by Osama bin Laden (pictured on page 17), the USA's most wanted man. Bin Laden supported the Al Qaeda attack on 11 September 2001, in which hijacked aeroplanes were crashed into US targets, killing 2,986 people.

Bin Laden claims that Al Qaeda has the right to attack the USA because it has troops in Arabia, a holy land for Muslims:

❝ The presence of the American crusader [Christian] armed forces in the countries of the Islamic Gulf is the greatest danger and the biggest harm that threatens the world's largest oil reserves.... The infidels must be thrown out of the Arabian Peninsula. ❞

An Afghan girl wanders through a refugee camp in Pakistan. Al Qaeda was based in Afghanistan at the time of the 9/11 attacks, but many Afghan Muslims fled from the extremist government there.

Stepping too far

In October 2001, after the attacks that killed so many people (some of them Muslims) the month before, bin Laden said:

❝ Our terrorism is a good, accepted terrorism because it's against America, it's for the purpose of defeating oppression so America would stop supporting Israel, [which] is killing our children. ❞

Muslim and non-Muslim people have joined together to condemn bin Laden. As one Muslim writer said:

❝ He has blasphemed Islam. He has used its sacred principles to incite murder and mayhem. He has declared war on the US and called on all Muslims to murder Americans, making Muslims targets for retaliatory attacks. He has exposed millions of Afghans to war, starvation and misery to save his own skin. If he were a hero, he would have surrendered. Not because he was guilty, but to save poor innocent Muslims from the ravages of war. ❞

DO CHRISTIAN EXTREMISTS CAUSE CONFLICT?

Across the world, some Christian leaders are still unwilling to live alongside different faiths. They use language that encourages people to think of other religions in terms of conflict.

Condemning Islam

Today, some Christian leaders are especially aggressive towards Muslims. The US Christian Reverend Jerry Falwell, for example, said on the *60 Minutes* TV show that Islam 'teaches hate' and that Mohammed was 'a terrorist'. Reverend Pat Robertson, founder of the Christian Coalition, said on the *Hannity and Colmes* show that Mohammed was:

" ...an absolute wild-eyed fanatic. He was a robber and a brigand. And to say that these terrorists distort Islam... they're carrying out Islam. I mean, this man [Mohammed] was a killer. "

The Reverend Jerry Falwell, speaking in 2005.

Christian extremists have strong views on many controversial subjects. Here, Spanish Christians protest in 2005 against the idea of same-sex marriages.

Religious fanaticism?

Some Christians want to force others to accept their views of other subjects, too. One man writing on a US Christian website objected to females playing sports. He said:

❝ Sport greatly hinders the development of godly, Biblical, feminine character.... I hope you will agree with me that we should keep our daughters away from competitive sports and spend our time training them how to be Biblically feminine women, wives and mothers. ❞

Some people feel that Christians are increasingly likely to use extreme methods to enforce their views. Another website correspondent feared that:

❝ Christian extremists are turning more and more to violence. Once placated by... gestures like having 'In God We Trust' stamped on coins, now they are turning to violence... [we should] show more concern over the rise of religious fanaticism. ❞

ANTI-ABORTION EXTREMISM

A Christian minister leads prayers at an anti-abortion protest in Buffalo, USA.

One issue that brings some Christians into conflict with other people is abortion. Abortion is when a woman decides not to allow the foetus that is growing in her body to be born. Instead, she deliberately ends her pregnancy.

Baby murder?

Christian anti-abortion protesters say that abortion is a form of murder because it ends a human life. In 1993, Dr David Gunn was shot and killed outside his clinic in Florida, USA. He worked there helping women to have abortions. Dr Gunn was shot dead by Michael Griffin, who later said:

❝ I asked the Lord what he wanted me to do.... I felt like I had... word from the Lord for [Dr Gunn]: that he was accused and convicted of murder and that his sentence was Genesis 9:6 'Whosoever sheds man's blood, by man his blood shall be shed'. ❞

ABORTION ATTACKS

Attacks and pickets said to have been made on abortion facilities

Year	Murders/Attempted Murders	Bombing, Arson, or Attempted	Pickets of Clinics
1989	0	11	72
1991	2	10	292
1993	2	20	2,279
1995	1	16	1,356
1997	2	16	7,518
1999	0	10	8,727
2001	0	5	9,969
2003	0	3	11,244

National Abortion Federation reports 'Incidents of Violence and Disruption Against Abortion Providers' in the USA and Canada

Free choice?

Most people object to the aggressive tactics that Christian anti-abortionists use. Some say that women should be free to make their own decisions about whether to have a baby or not:

❝ It's the ultimate irony that people who claim to represent a loving God resort to scare tactics and fear…. It's even worse when you consider that most women who have an abortion have just made the most difficult decision of their life. No one thinks abortion is a wonderful thing. No one tries to get pregnant just so they can terminate it. Even though it's not murder, it still eliminates a potential person, a potential daughter, a potential son. It's hard enough as it is. Women certainly don't need others telling them it's a murder. ❞

Paul Hill was a preacher who murdered an abortion clinician and was sentenced to death. Before his execution, he wrote: 'Much of the joy I felt after shooting the abortionist, and still feel today, is the joy of having freely obeyed Christ after long being enslaved to fearful obedience to men.'

HOW DO CULTS EMERGE?

In some religions, small groups of very dedicated followers appear. They follow their own version of the religion, usually based on the leader's views. Groups like this are sometimes called cults.

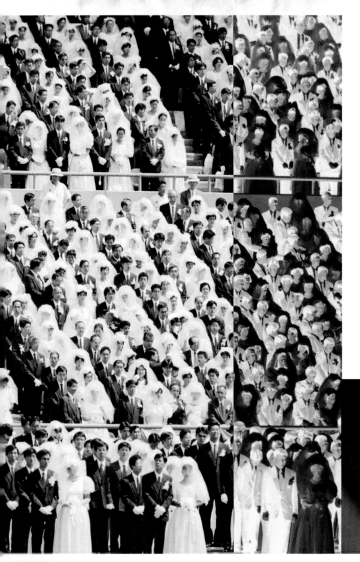

New recruits

Why are people tempted to join cults? Some people join because they want to live a different lifestyle; others want to do good work. One Christian group called The Family, for example, claims to be:

❝ ...an international Christian fellowship dedicated to sharing God's Word and love with others. [We] seek to comfort, help and minister to those in need, endeavouring to follow the model of Jesus. ❞

Once people become involved with cults, they sometimes find that things are not what they first seemed. One former cult member now says that:

❝ Looking back on my experience, I can say with great certainty that if I had known from the beginning what [it] was really all about, I would never have got involved – but that is simply not how cults operate. ❞

A mass wedding of followers of the Reverend Moon, who are often called 'Moonies'. Some of the couples may not even have met before, but marry out of obedience to their leader.

David Berg founded the cult known as The Children of God (now called The Family).

Inside activities

Cults often try to keep their activities partly secret from the outside world. The Family, for example, was once known as The Children of God. Its members were said to have used children for sex. Some went out 'flirty fishing' – looking for people who could be lured into the cult using sex. One former Family member remembers:

❝ When I was 15 or 16, we had a reporter come and stay with us. My mother asked me to take her for a meal and a drink. I was taught never to tell outsiders what happens, that they 'don't understand God's way'. My mother was pleased with me because this reporter went off and wrote a glowing article. ❞

Another ex-cult member says:

❝ As cults develop and become less open, they impose a mental stranglehold in their attempt to set the world view of their members in stone. ❞

"When you meet the friendliest people you have ever known, who introduce you to the most loving group of people you've ever encountered, and you find the leader to be the most inspired, caring, compassionate and understanding person you've ever met, and then you learn the cause of the group is something you never dared hope could be accomplished, and all of this sounds too good to be true – it probably is too good to be true! Don't give up your education, your hopes and ambitions to follow a rainbow."

Jeannie Mills, ex-member of The People's Temple, later found murdered.

ARE CULTS DANGEROUS?

Sometimes cults are so determined to follow their version of religion that they become highly isolated from the outside world. This can have disastrous results. Some cult members come into violent conflict with the authorities.

Under siege

In 1993, a conflict flared up between members of the Branch Davidian religion and government agents at Waco, Texas, USA. A gunfight broke out – four agents died and 16 were wounded, along with an unknown number of Davidians. The Davidian base was quickly besieged. David Koresh, the Davidian leader, refused to surrender. One investigator later said:

" For years, Koresh [had] been brainwashing his followers in this battle between the church and the enemy. [When the siege started] his prophecy came true. Koresh [convinced] his followers that the end [was] near, as he predicted. Their enemies [would] surround them and kill them. "

Floodlights illuminate the besieged Branch Davidian compound by night.

34

The Branch Davidian compound goes up in flames.

Meeting 'the end'

Almost two months later, the siege ended tragically. FBI agents tried to storm the base. A massive fire began, in which more than 70 Davidians died.

Some people say that the FBI had failed to understand how cult members think. The FBI had isolated the Davidians, confirming their idea that a battle with the authorities was inevitable. Koresh is claimed to have declared, 'We knew you were coming before you did.' One cult expert suggested that:

❝ By shining bright lights, playing loud music, [and] trying to deprive them of sleep [the FBI] reinforced the Davidians' views of an evil, Satanic outside world that was torturing them. They should have brought picnic baskets with fried chicken and soda pop and played Koresh's favorite music, instead of treating them like trapped rats. ❞

FAMOUS CULT MASS DEATHS

GROUP/YEAR	LOCATION	CIRCUMSTANCES/NUMBER DEAD
People's Temple Christian Church, 1978	Jonestown, Guyana	914 members of the cult found dead
Branch Davidian, 1993	Waco, Texas, USA	Siege by FBI ends with more than 70 Davidians dead
Order of the Solar Temple, 1994	Cheiry, Switzerland	48 cult members found dead in a farmhouse

CAN CULTISTS BECOME TERRORISTS?

Sometimes cults become so isolated from the real world that they make violent attacks on outsiders. One example of this is the Aum Shinrikyu cult in Japan.

Gas attack

In 1995, some Aum members released a deadly gas called sarin into the Tokyo subway. The attack killed 12 people and left thousands more injured. Yuli Kim, a South Korean living in Japan, was a 17-year-old student when she was affected by the attack and hospitalised for 11 days. Now 27, Kim says:

❝ My symptoms, such as having nightmares and fear of going to stations, subsided after two or three years, a bit quicker than some other people. What I'm doing now is trying to help fellow victims. ❞

Why did this attack happen? Why did Aum members want to attack ordinary Japanese people in this terrible way?

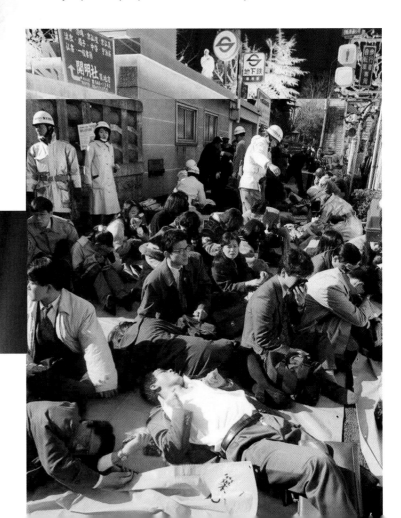

Victims of the 1995 gas attack are treated. Aum used the poison sarin, which attacks the body's nervous system and can cause people slowly to stop breathing and die.

A Japanese newspaper announces that the leader of Aum, Shoko Asahara, has been sentenced to death by hanging.

Justification?

For many, the Aum attack was an act of pure evil. But others explained it in another way. They believed the popularity of Aum (which now calls itself Aleph) had been caused by Japanese society. A writer on a Japanese website noted:

❝ Putting your employer, your money and your father's dream in first place is not a very satisfying life. A lot of people feel empty, heartless like robots. There is an imbalance. We must find a new, harmonious way for society. Or we see our sons becoming something very ugly. ❞

The Aum cult's philosophy was based on Buddhism combined with spiritual elements from other religions including Hinduism and Christianity. One young Japanese man said that cults have become popular because:

❝ The Japanese education system doesn't teach about spirituality. I'm sure that many young people are searching for how to live their lives better. ❞

COULD EXTREMISTS TAKE OVER?

In some countries, extremists have already taken over. In both Iran and, until 2001, Afghanistan, religious movements have been in charge of whole countries.

Taliban torment

In Afghanistan between 1996 and 2001, a group called the Taliban governed most of the country. The Taliban were, and remain, extremist Muslims. For example, women were not supposed to go out unaccompanied by a man. One female doctor remembered:

66 My husband hailed a taxi to take me... to the hospital. Five minutes later, a Religious Police car stopped the taxi.... There were three Taliban. I was scared. He asked me... why are you alone in the taxi? I asked, 'Are you going to beat me?' He beat me. I hid my face. He hit me several times on the back and arms. 99

The Taliban were overthrown by a US-led invasion in 2001.

After the fall of the Taliban, Afghan women could go out unaccompanied, shop and wear make-up for the first time. But despite their new freedom, many still hide their faces under burqas.

"Women have suffered massive, systematic, and unrelenting human rights abuses that have permeated every aspect of their lives.... Thousands of women have been physically assaulted and have had severe restrictions placed on their liberty and fundamental freedoms."
Humanity Denied: Systematic Violations of Women's Rights in Afghanistan, Human Rights Watch, 2001.

Canadian troops launch an attack during the invasion of Afghanistan. The invasion toppled the extremist Taliban party from power.

Western regimes

Some people have suggested that it is not only Muslims who seek to bring their religious views into government. One writer declared that:

“ Even as President George W Bush denounced the brutal Islamic fundamentalist regime in Kabul, he was quietly laying the foundations for his own fundamentalist regime at home. ”

Just to prove that you can never please everyone, though, other voters in the USA felt that President Bush was not religious enough in his views:

“ I hear a lot of Christians saying that they don't feel they can vote for President Bush. They... feel that he has abandoned the conservative Christian voters and has pandered to the moderate and even left-leaning voter. ”

WILL EXTREMISM EVER END?

Hinduism, Buddhism, Christianity and Islam – as well as many other religions – have all experienced extremism at some point in their history. Extremism has been in place for a very long time. Will it ever end?

Approaching Armageddon?

Some experts believe that conflicts between religious extremists are getting worse. As Benazir Bhutto, the former prime minister of Pakistan, said in 2004:

❝ There appear to be groups in both the Muslim and non-Muslim worlds who believe that a clash of civilisations is needed for religious reasons. ❞

Certainly today's hi-tech guns, deadly gases and other weapons mean that religious conflicts could kill more people than ever before. A British reporter in 2004 suggested:

❝ A clash of civilisations can lead to Armageddon, where there will be no winners on earth. But perhaps the religious extremists are not searching for winners on earth. ❞

Armed supporters of the extremist Muslim leader Moqtada al Sadr raise their weapons in Iraq in 2005.

"The proposition that my belief is threatened because you believe something else is not tenable. My belief is only threatened if you do something that threatens me personally or my co-believers. If nobody starts the trouble, we could do as our beliefs command us in perfect peace."

Dan Smith in *The State of the World Atlas*, 2003 edition.

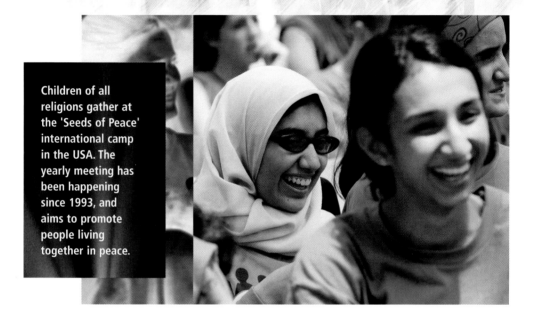

Children of all religions gather at the 'Seeds of Peace' international camp in the USA. The yearly meeting has been happening since 1993, and aims to promote people living together in peace.

Finding a way forward

Religion is involved in some of the world's most vicious conflicts. Some people feel that this makes it easy to identify the problem if only we dared. Among them is the controversial writer Salman Rushdie:

❝ We go on skating around this issue, speaking of religion in the fashionable language of 'respect'. What is there to respect in any of this [religious violence in India], or in any of the crimes now being committed almost daily around the world in religion's dreaded name? How well, with what fatal results, religion erects totems, and how willing we are to kill for them! So India's problem turns out to be the world's problem. What happened in India has happened in God's name. The problem's name is God. ❞

For others, religion has an important, healthy place in people's lives:

❝ Religion can comfort the afflicted. It can help survivors to once again discern some worthwhile structure in the universe. It can provide help in healing wounded spirits, and some lessons on how to avoid... violence and atrocity. It CAN do all these things – which is not to say that it always does them. ❞

WHERE DOES RELIGIOUS CONFLICT HAPPEN?

Religious extremists often come into conflict with members of other religions because they refuse to accept any challenge to their own 'true' faith. Examples of religious war and violence come from all around the world.

❶ Northern Ireland

Conflict between: Protestant and Catholic Christians
Since: 1920
Characteristics: physical assaults, bombings, shootings

❷ Bosnia and Kosovo

Conflict between: Christians and Muslims
Since: 1990s
Characteristics: mass executions, forced removal of people, fighting between armed groups

❸ Chechnya

Conflict between: Russian Christians and Muslim Chechens
Since: 1991
Characteristics: bombings, terrorist attacks in Russia (including Moscow and Beslan) by Chechen groups

❹ Iraq

Conflict between: Sunni Muslims and Shi'ite Muslims
Since: modern conflict began in 1960s
Characteristics: initially Sunni government persecution of Shi'ite Muslims; after a US-led invasion in 2003, Sunnis lost power and began a campaign of bombings and assassinations

"In January 2002 Chechen rebels included all Christians on their list of official enemies, vowing to blow up every church... in Russia."

Russia, Voice of the Martyrs.

A survivor of the 2004 Beslan school siege, where hundreds of Russian children and adults were shot by Muslim extremists.

❺ Israel
Conflict between: Jews and Arabs (mainly Muslim)
Since: modern conflict began in 1948
Characteristics: bombing attacks, shootings, destruction of homes

❻ Afghanistan
Conflict between: Taliban and non-extremists
Since: roughly 1979
Characteristics: beatings, shootings, bombings

❼ Pakistan/India/Bangladesh
Conflict between: Hindus and Muslims
Since: modern conflict began in 1947
Characteristics: riots, beatings, arson, sometimes massacres of groups of people

❽ Bali
Conflict between: Balinese Hindus and Javanese Muslims, and Muslim terrorists and the West

Since: tensions rose in 1990s
Characteristics: beatings, knifings, major bomb attacks in October 2002 and October 2005

❾ Ivory Coast
Conflict between: Christians and Muslims
Since: 2000
Characteristics: government forces have begun *"targeting [Muslim] civilians solely... on the basis of their religion."* Human Rights Watch, 2001

❿ USA
Attacks by: Christian extremists, Muslim terrorists
Since: 1990s
Characteristics: assaults, shootings, bombings

⓫ United Kingdom
Target of attacks by Muslim terrorists
Since: 2005
Characteristics: attacks by Muslim suicide bombers on civilian targets

Swords like this are rarely seen at political meetings. The former Indian prime minister (right) seems surprised to see one here.

TIMELINE

AD 313 The Roman Emperor Constantine legalises the previously banned Christian faith.

325 The Council of Nicaea is held by Roman Emperor Constantine, to decide a dispute between two sides of the Christian Church. The 'Aryans' lose the dispute and are driven underground.

c610 The prophet Mohammed begins to see visions he believes are messages from God. Over the next 22 years his visions are gathered together in a book called the Qur'an.

622 Mohammed founds the Islamic religion, of which the Qur'an is the holy book.

638 Arab forces take control of Jerusalem, in Palestine, where many Muslim, Christian and Jewish holy places are located.

656 The Battle of the Camel is fought between the forces of Ali (Mohammed's son-in-law) and Ayisha (one of his widows). It is the first battle between Muslims. In the end, Ali's supporters become what are today called Shi'ite Muslims. Other Muslims (the majority) become known as Sunni Muslims.

700s 'Moors' (Muslims from North Africa) conquer much of Spain.

1000–1492 Christian forces expel the Moors from Spain. Last to leave are the Moors of Granada, who surrender the city rather than see it destroyed. Some Muslims remain in the city.

1096–1270 European Christian countries organise the Crusades – eight military expeditions to win back Palestine, the Holy Land (much of which is now in Israel), from the Muslims.

1212 The Children's Crusade to Palestine takes place. Thousands of boys and girls from France and Germany embark on a pilgrimage to capture Jerusalem from Muslim control. None of the children reach the Holy Land. Many starve, drown or freeze to death; others return home or are sold as slaves by Muslims.

1550 All people in Granada, Spain, are ordered to be Christians. Non-Christians must leave the city. A few Muslim Moors convert to Christianity and become known as 'moriscos'.

1878 Jewish Zionists settle in Palestine. Zionists are Jews who believe they have a God-given right to reclaim the Holy Land.

1917   The Balfour Declaration: British politician Arthur Balfour says that Jewish people should have the right to settle in Palestine. (Britain governs Palestine at this time.)

1930s–1945 The Holocaust – forces under the control of Germany round up Jewish people, taking them to concentration camps where they are worked to death or killed.

1936   The Arab revolt: Muslim Arabs in Palestine revolt against the British, partly as a protest about Jewish immigration.

1947   India and Pakistan become independent countries, sparking months of violence between Hindus and Muslims.

1948   Israel's War of Independence: as the Jewish country of Israel is founded, it is attacked by Muslim countries. The Israeli forces win victory and Israel expands its territory. Thousands of Muslims flee from their homes and become refugees.

1967   The June War is fought between Israel and the Arabs.

1971   India helps East Pakistan in a war against West Pakistan. East Pakistan becomes an independent country, Bangladesh.

1972   Palestinian terrorists take 11 Israeli athletes hostage at the Olympic Games. Two are killed immediately; the other nine, as well as five terrorists and a policeman, are killed in a later gun battle.

1973   The October War is fought between Israel and the Arabs.

1984   Indian Prime Minister Indira Gandhi (a Hindu) is assassinated by members of the Sikh religion.

1991   Former Indian Prime Minister Rajiv Gandhi is assassinated by Tamil Tigers.

1994–1996, 1999 onwards Russian forces engage in war with Chechen rebels in Chechnya. Most Chechens are Muslim, most Russians Christian.

2001   Muslim terrorists attack New York, USA, using hijacked passenger aircraft. The USA and its allies launch an attack on Afghanistan, believed to be sheltering Osama bin Laden. The extremist Taliban are toppled, but bin Laden is not captured.

2003   Muslim terrorists detonate bombs in Bali, Indonesia, killing 200 holidaymakers. Indonesia is mainly Muslim, but Bali is Hindu and popular with Western tourists.

2005   Muslim suicide bombers target the London transport system, killing 52 people. Another Muslim bomb explodes in Bali.

GLOSSARY

anti-Semitism Dislike of Jewish people because they are Jewish.

anti-social Describing behaviour that is likely to annoy, offend or hurt other people.

Armageddon A word from the Christian Bible, describing the battle between the forces of good and evil that will mark the end of the world.

besieged Surrounded by armed forces, which are aiming to force a surrender.

blaspheme To treat God or sacred things in a way that will be offensive to religious people.

brainwashing Wiping out a person's previous views and replacing them with new ones that they have not developed themselves.

brigand A robber or highwayman.

concentration camps Camps where enemies are collected together in poor conditions, in the hope that they will die or to kill them.

crusader A Christian fighter who fought Muslims in the Holy Land during the Middle Ages.

cynical Unlikely to take anything on trust; naturally disbelieving.

divine To do with God.

ethnic cleansing Removing or killing a whole group of people – for example Muslims or Gypsies – from a particular area.

fratricidal Literally, killing your own brother. Today people use this word to describe the act of killing someone you are close to.

Gaza Strip An area of land in Israel whose ownership is especially hotly disputed between Israelis and Palestinians.

genocide Deliberate killing of a whole people.

heretics People who do not follow the accepted version of a religion.

holocaust The killing of Jews and others by the German Nazis and their supporters before and during the Second World War.

jihad A Muslim holy war or holy fight.

lynching Illegal 'punishment' for alleged crimes, often by hanging or burning the 'offender'.

morality Ways of behaving – such as respecting others – that are thought of as being right and proper.

patron saint A saint who is associated with a particular place or people.

pyre A stack of wood, often one used to burn a dead body.

racism Treating someone differently because of his or her racial background.

sacred Holy or linked to religion.

spirituality Belief to do with a person's soul or spirit, rather than material things.

suicide bombers People who deliberately blow themselves up in order to kill or maim others too.

war crimes Illegal acts that were committed during a war.

RESOURCES

Books

Reference and non-fiction
For younger readers
Encyclopedia of Religion by Philip Wilkinson, Rabbi Douglas Charing (Dorling Kindersley, 2004)
Explains the beliefs of the world's main religions, as well as where most of their followers are based.

The Oxford Children's A–Z of World Religions by Anita Ganeri (Oxford University Press, 2004)
Allows readers to check the meaning and significance of a variety of religious beliefs and practices.

What Would Buffy Do?: The Vampire Slayer as Spiritual Guide by Jana Riess (Jossey Bass Wiley, 2004)
A light-hearted look at some of the morality in the TV show *Buffy The Vampire Slayer*. Focuses on the need for humour in fighting spiritual battles.

The Muslim Experience by J F Aylett, Kevin O'Donnell (editor) (Hodder Arnold H&S, 2000)
Describes the experience of being a Muslim.

For older readers
The Freedom to Do God's Will: Religious Fundamentalism and Social Change by James Busuttil (editor), Gerrie Ter Haar (editor) (Routledge, 2002)
A collection of articles on the motivations and causes of religious extremism.

Fiction
For older readers
The Kite Runner by Khaled Hosseini (Bloomsbury, 2004)
The story of a young Muslim boy growing up in Afghanistan, the rise of the Taliban, and his move to the USA.

The Bookseller of Kabul by Asne Seierstad (Virago, 2004)
An account of life in Kabul, the capital city of Afghanistan, after the fall of the Taliban. The book concentrates on life for the women of one family.

Zanzibar by Giles Foden (Faber and Faber, 2003)
The fictional story of how a terrorist attack by Muslim extremists develops on an island off the coast of Africa.

Films

The Battle for Algiers directed by Gillo Pontecorvo, 1965 (Certificate 15)
The disturbing story of how the French forces that at the time controlled Algeria put down a Muslim uprising in Algiers, the capital city. Despite showing violence from both sides, the film was banned in France when it was released. *The Battle for Algiers* is said to have been shown to officials in the USA at the time of the invasion of Afghanistan, as a demonstration of how to win a battle but lose the support of local people.

INDEX